Contents

Kirkby	6
Saint Kevin's	24
In a Catholic Style	43
The Teachers	55
The Boys	84
Sex and the single school boy	96
This sporting life	107
Academic Affairs	113
Epilogue: the escape	122

'Why should I not publish my memories of school? I have often seen reminiscences of people who's schools I have never even heard of, and I fail to see -- because I do not happen to be a 'Somebody' -- why my memories should not be interesting.' Paraphrased from Charles Pooter, 1888

It has occurred to me that I know perhaps more than I would like to know about other people's schools. For a start, through film and TV I know, at least in skeleton form, how to manage my way through life in American schools. I have worried about whether or not characters I have never met will get a date for the junior prom. I know what a corsage is and who gets one. I know that the corridor which contains the school lockers is where a) the school bully hangs out with his sidekicks, ready to nick your lunch money or b) you get a contemptuous look from the mean cheerleader and her fellow harpies.

For British schools my main sources of familiarity have come from the accounts of other people; Billy Bunter, Tom Brown, the Winslow Boy and others. These were schools where the pupils never went home, except when the school actually closed at Christmas or summer. This is a world where there are half holidays. They are schools where young boys cry themselves to sleep because mummy hasn't written, again. Where the food is so bad that the boys resort to events called midnight feasts in the dorms, often involving the fruit cake mummy had sent, by post, from home. Rugger, cold showers and misery at the hands of Forbes major.

Of my own experience of life in a single sex, single religion, single class, council estate comprehensive school there is relatively little depicted on screen or in literature. Grange Hill, possibly. Derry girls, yes (ish). Also there were the odd excursions such as 'Our Day Out' and 'Kes' which featured schools like mine at least as a backdrop to a broader plot.

This is a pity. Our school was a unique and largely successful experiment in the education of boys from a very special town and at a very special time. From the mid 1960s to the early 1970s I shared an education system which, for all its drawbacks (and there were many), still retained an optimism about the future and our place in it. Bright, clean, warm and modern our school aimed to play its part in the white heat of social change that was all the rage in Harold Wilson's Britain.

What follows is what I remember about school in Saint Kevins. I don't claim that this is an accurate historical record of the period or of the school itself and I don't care if I have made mistakes. As I grow older, many of the facts are becoming dimmer and I am conscious that I might be recalling events through a rosy glow of nostalgia. But I don't care, these are my memories and if you find any inaccuracies, sue me. Or write to your MP.

All the photos in the text are courtesy of the Knowsley archive in the towny. My heartfelt thanks to their lovely staff.

Chris

marmadukestreet2022@gmail.com

Kirkby

"It was good. My mum and dad thought this was the great new world that came but they did have some doubts when they moved in and had talks about moving back to Liverpool. But when St Kevin's school opened my dad went to go see it and saw all science labs and facilities. He knew if we stayed we'd get a good education." Jeff Morris, moved to Kirkby, 1958

What must the original farmers of Kirkby have thought? It had been bad enough during the war, becoming neighbours with enormous ordnance factories. One major accident in these, and you could say goodbye to your little stone built cottage. Ten percent of all the bullets used in the conflagration came from these factories, apparently, and I doubt any one of the villagers were ever asked what they thought of their explosive neighbour. In the 1960s you could still see clearly what was left of the production facilities. There was no shortage of war-time architecture to be seen in Kirkby. Within view of our house on Simonswood Lane was a gun emplacement built with walls of reinforced concrete a couple of feet thick. These were great for growing kids to play in, if you could tolerate the whiff of human doings which always seemed to envelop these structures. Building the bombs and bullets which won the war was not the only service this part of Kirkby delivered to the nation. The repurposed war factories became one of the country's new 'industrial estates'. Kirkby was all about post war planning, big state intervention and jobs-for-all which was pretty much how things panned out for many years. But the further service Kirkby rendered to the nation was in the breaking up of the wartime stuff that was now surplus to requirements. There was a huge yard on the estate which stored wartime aeroplane cockpits waiting to have their internal organs harvested as scrap. It was known to the local kids as the 'aery dump' and even though the cocky watchman did his best to keep us out, it could be easily accessed over the fence. Inside, piled high like cars at a scrapyard, the cockpits were at your disposal. Take your pick. Pull the spitfire levers back. Press the pedals if you could reach them. Look at the dials. This stuff would probably be worth a fortune now but then it was next to worthless, except for us kids. We loved the place. You could understand why the authorities wanted to keep us out. It was a death trap and I can't imagine that the owners of the site were overburdened by insurance in case any kids got injured while they were illegally at play. It was an era of light touch regulation. My mum would have killed me if she had known I was there, not that any of us would have told our mums.

Lots of people in Kirkby worked in the repurposed factories left over from the war. My mum made TV and radio valves in Dubiliers and later she made iced cream and lolly ices in Pendleton's: "What could be nicer than a Pendleton's twicer?"

There was also a large coffin factory on the estate. Was this also part of the war effort? Did the factory provide the last accommodation for the lads who never made it home from the fighting? Or the families who never survived the blitz? None of these questions occurred to us as kids, and why should it? It has never occurred to me to wonder about it until I came to write these lines. All we saw was a coffin factory with seemingly unlimited supplies of off cut wood for the bonfires of November 5, universally known as 'bommy'. Later on it became the source of materials for go carts, universally known as 'steeries'. These were crudely assembled wooden frames, courtesy of the coffin factory, loosely attached to wheels which had been cannibalised from the sort of large wheeled prams that were in every home in Kirkby throughout the 1960s. There was no shortage of pram spare parts to be had. A pram carcass was a regular feature of any fly tipping site. The combination in Kirkby of youthful tenantry, lads coming home from war and fresh country air meant that small children were everywhere. The huge numbers of Catholics transported from bombed out Liverpool meant that, in theory at least, population growth was guaranteed. Also, besides the pub and the church, there wasn't much else for the young population of the town to do besides procreate. A photo taken of Kirkby in the 1960s shows a Woolworths with a veritable car park of these prams outside the shop, their mewling and puking inmates left unattended while the housewives went in for their Oxydol and Omo. You could do that in those days and nobody would bat an eyelid. It seems odd now. It seems odder still that the women of the town had so much time on their hands. During the day, the men disappeared from the streets and Kirkby became a city of women, bescarfed and I guess, bored stiff. It was a long time before there was even a library.

But I digress. What must the yeomanry of the tiny village have made of the Kirkby Newtown development? Every contact we had with the aboriginal population of the area convinced you of one thing. They were country mice and we were town mice, even if we were born in Kirkby. Their village with it's slow, soft, Lancashire accent was suddenly, very suddenly, overrun by fast talking scousers you had to keep your eye on. We had a farm opposite our house, close to the little tree, for those of you who knew the area. It was occupied by, in my memory, people who looked like they'd stepped from a Raymond Briggs cartoon, all grandma aprons and grandad braces with a pipe. Their homely appearance didn't save them from us kids, aged six or seven, from pestering them with commando raids in search of blackcurrants from their garden. We knew them as 'dog berries' for some reason. The words 'culture shock' can scarcely cover the impact that the importation of fifty thousand people from the slummy, war devastated streets of downtown Liverpool must have had on the rustics. They still lived in houses of sandstone and their kids attended schools with an open fire. It must have been like the 'Railway Children' meets 'Cathy Come Home'. And yet I don't recall any hostility from them. Perhaps I was too young to pick it up.

My own mum and dad had been 'decanted', from a flat above a chippy on Park Road in the Dingle that had gone on fire. My mum had to get me out of the place before I myself, her only child, was deep fried with the fish. She always suspected that the chip shop owner had had a hand in the conflagration in order to escape to Speke of all places. Things were that bad.

Whisperings in the family suggested that Bill and Sal (my mum and dad) had somehow bent the housing allocation rules to get their house in Kirkby. Who checked the paperwork when an entire population was on the move? Be realistic. So, in 1958, we were decanted to Kirkby. *To decant; verb, "gradually pour (wine, port, or another liquid) from one container into another, typically in order to separate out sediment".* The decanting process took us to Simonswood Lane, number 123 which made remembering the address easy. The ability to remember my address was drilled into me from an early age. The Kirkby of the 1960s was an area of low car ownership and high kiddy density. People wax nostalgically about this period but in our case it was true: kids roamed. We roamed extensively and from an early age too. Our parents didn't have to take us to school, and we would have rejected any suggestion that they bring us. Walking to school was mates' time. The idea of being brought to school by your mum would have been suicide for your playground reputation. Even girls came with their mates. It was one of the first skills my mum taught me. How to know your address if you got lost. There were other skills she couldn't teach me. One was how to navigate the local dogs. This was an era where dog management consisted of opening the door in the morning and saying 'ta ta' to the mongrel (and it was always mongrels) till it decided to come home. The streets were full of them, neatly arranged in packs. My mum was never a fan of dogs but even she had to admire them in the street: 'Have you ever noticed how dogs always look as though they are going somewhere?'. You only ever see dogs on leads these days. In Kirkby in the 1960s they used to chase after cars. I don't think they had thought through what they would do if they caught one.

1958, the year of my first memories, I think. Billy (dad) 29 and Sally (mum) 26, from living above a chippy where they always smelled of chips to being the first tenants in a brand new council house with an inside toilet and a bath (first time) and a garden back and front. As if this wasn't enough there were fields directly opposite our house with miles of open countryside leading to the industrial estate where people went to work. There were thousands of them by foot and on overcrowded buses, the 92 as I recall. There was a massive hubbub between 08.00 and 09.00. Then it was quiet. Then massive hubbub between 04.30 and 05.30. Then it was quiet. My dad never got over his sense of gratitude and pride in this house and resisted any suggestions that we move or buy the place until old age and Parkinson's disease reduced to nothing his power to resist. He was gratefully overspilled into the countryside and spent his leisure hours winning council prizes for the quality of his garden. His idea of a day out with the kids was to go around eyeing the competition for the coveted awards and giving due credit to the quality of someone else's pelargoniums. I still know the addresses of his keenest rivals. And for me, a three year old, carried over the threshold of this paradise regained, the luxury of this accommodation was all I was ever to know. The smell of fresh, wettish plaster still brings a recollection of those days. The houses on the next block were not yet finished and were still being built. It was all Sally could do to keep the mud of the building sites out of her lovely new home.

It wasn't just the numbers of people who descended on the Lancashire crossroads that was the hamlet of Kirkby in the 1950s. It was also the demographics. Droves of hormone ravaged young newlyweds, half of whom were supposed to have an ideological objection to birth control, descended on the Newtown. Very quickly the population began to bulge in a notable way. This was not a process peculiar to Kirkby, it was all over the country. This was the birth of the boomer generation. It's just that in Kirkby the phenomenon took on an exaggerated and some might say grotesque aspect. Kirkby at one point was said to have the highest square mile concentration of under twenty ones in Europe. The adults were swamped by the kids. Kids were everywhere and seemed to be multiplying like a runaway atomic chain reaction. Two illustrations of this spring to my mind. Across the field opposite our house was a Birds Eye factory. This used to take vegetables from the surrounding countryside and turn them into blocks of ice. Peas 'as fresh as when the pods went pop' as the TV advert used to say. They transported the peas in lorries and, so poorly packed were the lorries, the peas would hang over the sides in insanely large numbers. Kids used to line the roads with sticks and, like little guerillas, would ambush the transport by hooking the peas from the lorries. Then we would sit and eat the sweet contraband by the side of the road until the next van arrived. Kids eating fresh veg, who'd have thought it? When I tasted frozen peas many years later I had a 'fresh wettish plaster' moment, recalling the days we risked our necks for peas. Tinned peas just don't taste the same.

But I digress. One time some big wig from the Birds Eye corporation came to the town and arrived in a helicopter. Helicopters were not as common in the 1960s as they are today. If you saw a helicopter in the sky you would point at it. It was like a UFO. And one of them landed in our field. This was astonishing in itself. But the point I am trying to make is this. Within seconds, literally seconds, thousands of kids emerged as if from nowhere and streamed spontaneously onto the field to stare at this...apparition. The numbers were staggering but then the number of kids on the streets of Kirkby at any one time were staggering.

The second illustration of the numbers of kids in Kirkby happened in 1964. I know this date because the event has been widely referenced online, look it up for yourself. A rumour went around the kids of the town that leprechauns had been seen in Saint Chads church in Kirkby town centre, or the 'towny' as it is universally known. Me and the seven lads I went around with (seven lads under 12 from six houses, two of which contributed no lads at all. You do the maths) all went to investigate. After all, there were pots of gold at stake. Very soon we were carried along on a tsunami of kids all on the lookout for the little people. Naturally, none were found but this lesson was not driven home before every last scrap of vegetation had been torn up searching for them. This was the leprechaun panic of '64. I don't recall seeing anyone in authority. It wouldn't surprise me to learn that the only adults on the scene were the entrepreneurial ice cream vendors who turned up in their vans.

The skewing of the population towards the under aged brought with it problems, as you can imagine. The adults were swamped. Law and order was overwhelmed, but in a way that was almost quaint by modern 'stabby' standards. In this period the authorities laid on 'Police Houses'. These were clearly identifiable homes for police officers with, I think, blue lights outside the front door. I think that this scheme didn't last long.

People would have their homes broken into for the loose change that their electricity meters contained. Phone boxes barely lasted a week before they had their hand pieces pulled off. It was a criminologist's paradise. We even had our own crime series on TV. Z Cars, the premier UK cop show of its era, was not so loosely based on Kirkby, or 'Newtown' in the show. All the big stars of the day were in it. Stratford Johns, Frank Findlay, James Ellis (who brought a neat Irish touch to the show) and Brian Blessed. I don't know if I am remembering this correctly, but I get the feeling that the opening sequence featured a picture of the doorway of a Kirkby pub.

The reputation of the town for a time was, shall we say, unenviable. In the 60s one of the colour supplements - Observer or Sunday Times - ran an item about Kirkby and presented a series of pictures to support the article. But they were all in black and white. In a colour supplement. Even as a youth I was aggrieved; why us? Give us a break!

One problem that did not come with the decanted population was religious sectarianism. The religious rivalries that Liverpool had been famous for did not travel well. You could see the ancient structures of the conflict easily enough, but it was in a petrified form and its fire had gone out. Early on there were half hearted attempts to resurrect Catholic and Protestant identities. The 12th of July was observed albeit in muted form and the Catholics organised Whit Walks for many years but the heat had gone out of the conflict. A widely held view was that the mixing of the religions and the next door neighbourliness of Catholics and protestants was the last gift of the retreating Luftwaffe. I don't believe I ever saw any evidence of sectarian hostility. There was a keenly Orange family up our road. Mr Billy _____ had all the accoutrements of Orangeism on view in his house. He was an odd looking bloke who had the appearance of one of Benny Hill's characters: Fred Scuttle. He had a motorbike and sidecar and his house was full of motor bike parts. You could tell because the door was always open. I can't imagine how he got his wife to put up with it. My main memory of him was of a portly man in a vest who had a face that only a mother would love. One of our neighbours used to refer to him as Tyrone Power, in ironic honour of the Hollywood heart throb. But say what you like about Mr William of Orange, he would be good for fixing our Catholic bikes and he never did anybody any harm.

Where there was religious division was in the education system. The Catholics went one way and everyone else went in another, miscellaneous direction. Looking back, we were very lucky in the provision of our schools. Our families had left behind slum schools; leaky, cold, dark Victorian piles with poor resources and outside toilets. Our primary schools in Kirkby were out of the box brand new and looked like the schools in Ladybird books. Light, warm and well stocked, all they lacked was Janet and John.

When I saw the Ladybird version of school with fresh-faced teachers and children gazing at rounded letters on a blackboard, this was the world I knew. The schools of Bunter books, with their midnight feasts in the dorms, were unknown to me, thank God. Half holiday? They sound OK but what in tarnation are they?

Half the kids in the town went to the state schools and half to the Catholic schools. At secondary school the feeders sent kids four ways. The state school kids went to the mixed schools Roughwood and Brookfield. The Catholic kids were further segregated by sex. Boys went to St Kevin's, girls went to St Gregory's. All the schools were enthusiastically comprehensive.

Looking back on the period, it was no small achievement that the schools managed to organise the kids of the town so well. Each of the secondary schools imprisoned upwards of two thousand kids for the duration of the working day, and in that time taught the kids how to read, maths, languages, crafts, sports and literature. I went to Saint Kevins Roman Catholic Comprehensive School, and these were my sins.

Saint Kevin's

"I'm not saying our school was hard, but it had its own coroner" John Cooper Clark

In Saint Maries junior school everyone knew everyone else, and the school population was in the low hundreds. Leaving its welcoming bosom was a wrench. No, say it like it was, it was terrifying. From being the oldest kids in the school, the school elite, to being plunged into a dog fight of two thousand rough, tough boys caused me no end of anxiety. Two thousand! I, we, all of us were mortified. There were rumours of what we might expect. Ugly rumours. New kids stood out, with their new uniforms and their satchels and their shiny shoes. But nothing happened and after a few weeks, Saint Maries was a distant, if wistful, memory. Kids being what they are, I adapted and after the first month it was mostly plain sailing. Nobody bothered me and when I was an older kid I never even noticed the new kids as they arrived. There was too much going on.

The structure of the school was based on a house system. I don't know if this was in conscious imitation of public and grammar schools or if it is the natural way to organise large schools. The other schools had similar structures I think. The houses were named after stars in the Catholic firmament: Fisher (my own house), Bede, Newman, Aquinas, Aloyisius, Campion, Augustine and Gregory. The teachers tried their best to spirit up some inter house rivalry along the lines of Harry Potter houses, but I don't think anyone's heart was in it. 'Come on! Do it for Fisher house!!' Nah, not really. The main function of the house halls was registration, assembly and to act as dining halls. Assemblies consisted of prayers, a homily from one of the staff which relied on 'Eleanor Rigby' or 'Streets of London' too often for comfort, and contact with a mixed stream 'tutorial group'. This was a totally different group of lads from those in class. This was where we met lads from other streams, often for religious lessons. I'm not sure how well this forced mixing worked to be honest.

The school staff rooms were situated in each of the house halls. They were tiny and you would only ever consider knocking on the door of the staff room if you were actually on fire because the reception was not exactly welcoming. Mind you, the atmosphere in the staff rooms was toxic in the most literal sense of the word. Cigarette smoke would come pouring out of the tiny enclosed space in volumes that, today, a firefighter would baulk at.

For all the kids in Kirkby the normal option was to go comprehensive. We came from a domestic monoculture of council housing into an educational monoculture of equitable comprehensive schooling. Political debates and arguments raged on and on about comprehensive vs grammar schools but in our case the debate was over. We never knew anything else. Well this isn't exactly true. One kid, Michael Gower, who used to come first in every exam ever held in my primary school disappeared from view at secondary school. Apparently he went to a Catholic grammar school somewhere, I think it was St Edwards. None of his mates were envious of him. He'd be separated from his mates and have to travel miles while we lived a hop skip and a jump from school. Michael was an interesting character. Bright as a button, he lived in a flat with his grandmother who was from Austria, maybe Vienna. He could speak

German like a natural and would do so on request in the playground. I couldn't come close to matching that. The best I could do was to count to ten in Welsh. My mum taught me how. She had been a refugee in Anglesey during the war and had Welsh as her first language for a number of years. Counting to ten was all she had left in the 1960s, and she taught me how to do it. I can still do it. The trouble was that when I tried my party trick in the playground I discovered that lots of other kids could too. Their parents had taught them. Pride goes before a fall.

But I digress. Michael was the only sniff we had of selective education. I wonder what happened to him. I have some vague recollection of doing some kind of 11 plus type exam at around the time of 'going up' to St Kevs. You know the sort of thing: 'apple is to dog the way that ship is to -----', or 'If a bath is being filled with water, how big is the hole?' Puzzles like that baffled me then and baffle me now and I am not confident that I would ever have passed the 11 plus. But mostly for us, the transition to senior school did not have the terrors of the 11 plus that blighted the lives of so many of our age group elsewhere. This did not mean that there was no selection. The classes were set down in a pattern which was based on academic ability, but how this was defined was never clear, to me anyway. The scale just before we arrived went like this. The 'academic' streams were furthest to the left: Classes: P.A.X.D.O.M.I.N.E. Catholic classicists will understand this Latin phrase: 'the Peace of the Lord'. By the time we got to St Kevs this system had been abbreviated to: P (1-4), A(1-4), X (1-4) and D (1-4). In the first year I was put into class P2. I think that I had underperformed in maths in the 4th year of juniors. But quickly I joined the lads in P1.

As in primary school everything in St Kevs was brand new. The school was officially opened in 1966 by our local MP and then prime minister Harold Wilson, pipe and all. Fancy that! There was a plaque in the school reception commemorating the event. I wonder what happened to that plaque when the school was pulled down? In fact, the school had been unofficially opened many years before 1966 and already had launched numerous sets of old boys into the world. This wasn't the last time that Harold Wilson visited our school. On another occasion he came to give a speech to our sixth form. Blah blah blah, platitude platitude then came the questions. He gave a really interesting response to the question 'What are you most proud of in your premiership?'. His reply was, as I recall, without hesitation: 'The Open University'. I could see then, the thread of principle that ran from the OU directly to our new, comprehensive, all embracing school. More questions! One of the lads asked 'When will you implement clause 4 of the Labour Party constitution and start nationalising industries?'. The PM's response to this was suitably woolly. What was he to say? Even in your school hall the press and, beyond them, the markets would be watching. He wouldn't want to start a run on the pound from Fisher's house hall. So, moving on, more questions! Imagine the icy stares of the teachers when the same lad asked him the exact same question, heavy with the insinuation that his first question had not been answered. It must have come as some relief when one of the, shall we say, less controversial members of our group, asked the question 'What about Malta?'. This question resulted from a two day furore that had been rumbling in the press. The Wilson government wanted to reduce its military presence in Malta to save money and the Maltese didn't like it. But the question was so ill formed and obscure, for a time it became our go-to question for any teacher we wanted to undermine: 'Any questions lads?' 'Yes. What about Malta?' 'Yea? Very funny, sonny boy'.

The truth of the matter is that I don't think we realised just how well provisioned our school was. It was brand new and deluxe, except, oddly, it had a tiny car park. Our history teacher Tom Moynihan had a story relating to school car parks. He was one of those teachers who had lots of insightful stories. He said that in the austerity 1950s people would go to the cinema and see American films which depicted teenagers driving their own vehicles. This was seen as being so unlikely that, he said, there would be spontaneous outbreaks of laughter in the audience. In the first school that he got a job, he said, 'there was only one person who had any motorised transport and that was the headmaster. And he had a motorbike and sidecar'.

Our school lacked the campus style architectural elegance of Roughwood, the state school along the road. It also lacked the girls. But with its own swimming pool, tennis courts, acres of land for sports, an Olympic size running track for God's sake, woodwork and metal workshops, we were living in an educational nirvana. The school even had a Victorian faux castle behind it. It had been a water tower for the pre Newtown community but it was now redundant. One day during double physics, they blew the thing up. They didn't even warn us it would happen. I nearly jumped out of my skin.

The school biology department had all sorts of sad looking animals in it. They all looked as though they were waiting for a letter from the Home Office to release them. This included a caged monkey called Jacko. The purpose of keeping a monkey in chokey like this is hard to fathom. What had the monkey ever done to us? I can't see that it would be tolerated these days. In partial compensation for the injustice of its predicament the boys used to nick locusts from the locust cage (we had them too) and feed them to the captive through the bars. He would eat them with a satisfying crunching noise. I think that was the only fun it ever got, apart from its periodic escapes.

I have met many, many people who's parents sent them to very expensive public schools which had none of our resources and whose best offer was giving their boys an interest in the sort of minority erotic pastimes that seem to interest Tory MPs.

It's hard to speak of the other streams, but in our stream there were about 25 lads. When the stream divided up for GCEs the classes became smaller and by sixth form, my A level class for French consisted of me and two other lads. The other two didn't finish the course, I think one of them left school half way through sixth form. But I ended up with a teacher to myself. I can only imagine the arguments that must have taken place behind the scenes to justify this spending. But it is a marker of the optimism of the time, of the commitment to social democratic egalitarianism that this was thought to be justifiable.

The school day at St Kevs would start with assembly and registration (and prayers). Then everyone would go their own way to their own lessons. These would start and end with prayers, depending on the teacher. There was no open atheism from the staff but, you know, you got a feel for who were the super enthusiasts for religion and who were not. By the time that the cigarette smokers among the kids and the staff were becoming uncomfortable lungwise, there would be a break. In terms of layout the school was constructed as a series of blocks which surrounded a number of top quality tennis courts in the centre. The dream of a tennis playing democracy never actually came off but the tennis courts remained, falling further and further into disrepair. They started off as professional grade courts, surrounded by 12 foot plasticated fencing designed to keep in the balls that never got played. The kids just used to hang around in them during play times, playing footy and swearing. By the time we left they resembled nothing more than an exercise yard in a prison.

As in most schools there was an active tobacco den behind the bike sheds. The bike sheds were never, ever, used for bikes. Nobody would have been mad enough to leave an actual bike there. It was the sort of mad optimism about human nature that gave Kirkby its police houses. Has there ever been a sociological survey of why the bike sheds were universally the venue for shady behaviour? In St Kevs the smoking area was clearly marked. Someone had taken the time and trouble to paint 'Smokers Union' on one of the walls in case anyone got lost. That it was called a union at all indicated just how far the collectivist ideology of the 60s had penetrated our junior sensibilities. Today it would probably be called the 'Smokers Hedge Fund'. Anyway, it wasn't just the smoking that went on in the SU. This was also the nexus of the school's gambling industry. At every break time there would be boys playing a variety of games with coins. There was the classic odds and evens. This was a game of pure chance and even the best players could still lose their dinner money in the twinkling of an eye. More skill based was 'Nearest the Wall' where old style, pre decimal pennies would be thrown against a wall and the closest to the wall won the entire pot. This was a highly skilled game and my mate was one of the best at it. In fact he practically ran the whole operation and would frequently go home with pockets bulging, having relieved other lads of their ciggy money.

Lunch time was its own set of ritualised behaviours, not the least of which were the prayers before and after eating. As in so many other aspects of life at St Kevs things were ordered in what appeared to be a risible imitation of public school life. There was the 'Top Table' for the teachers. Running perpendicular to the top table, the house hall would be divided into 'Tables'. Each Table had eight boys. At the head of each table was a boy, usually but not exclusively an older boy. It was his job to dish out the dinners for the rest of the boys. What could possibly go wrong, eh? Mostly the dinners would go off with fair(ish) shares for the boys. But woe betide you if you fell out with the server. When the dinners had been distributed the tables started to resemble the trading floor in a stock exchange with lads lowerdown the table swapping sausages for potatoes, whatever. If you liked prunes you were made. They were a low value item and you could hoover up unwanted prunes to a bowel tormenting degree. The number of stones ringing a plate became an item of competition among the prune fanciers. One time I think I racked up twenty four in one sitting. Beat that, Bede house!

Because dinner time was organised on a house rather than a stream basis, you got to mix with lads outside your normal crew. The Table community was usually a fixed social order where kids started at the bottom and moved up towards a serving position. Some tables were more popular than others and a soprano cry of 'You get starved on this table' was not uncommon from the less popular dining slots. But for the kids who didn't fit in, life was not so straightforward. They could never get a toe hold in the social hierarchy of a table and would spend months going from the lowest rung of each table's ladder. An anthropologist could have written books about it.

After dinner (NB, dinner, not lunch. And certainly not 'luncheon') the dining tables were put away. Or were put away partially, the hall was then transformed for table tennis. We didn't use proper tables obviously, but the tables we had just eaten on, two tables for each side.

The split down the middle of the table would cause the ball to bounce unpredictably. This was regarded as an act of God and was built into our version of the rules. We didn't have proper bats, obviously, so we used hard backed textbooks. Particularly valued were the Latin books. They were both thin and hard backed. Nets were unheard of so we used the blazers our mothers had saved up for, all rolled up. This could result in a ball coming to a full stop on the net. What are the rules in that instance, I wonder? Generally we only had the cheapest of balls (called, by us, 'floaters') and these would bounce off the joins in the table at right angles to its direction causing the boy losing a point to cry 'jammy bastard'. When the bell rang for the start of the afternoon assembly the boys were IN THEORY supposed to put the tables away to make room for the multitude on their way back in from milling around or gambling. But in FACT when the bell rang everyone scarpered for the door. This was an every day occurrence and was as predictable as a tide. One time, my gambling supremo mate took a cleaners broom which had been left out and jammed it between the handles of the house hall door after the first bell rang. Predictably the stampede for the door occurred, right on cue but of course the doors wouldn't open. Through the window in the door we could see boys piling up against the door in blind panic at the thought that they might have to put away the tables that, five minutes ago, they had been playing on. When he saw the havoc that his broom handle had induced, he lost his nerve and pulled it out with one rapid tug. The panicked masses now tumbled out into a heap on the floor. I don't believe I have ever laughed as much at anything in my life.

Discipline in St Kevins was simple and direct. It was run on a bizarre accounting system that involved the teachers assigning a 'bill' to a boy. This would be issued by the offended teacher and distributed as an invoice back to the boy's house master. He was then expected to take an eighteen inch piece of leather, a quarter of an inch thick, and wallop the hands of the homework dodger or uniform dissident. This he did cold, without the frustration or anger of the teacher who had issued the bill. The names of the offenders would be read out to the house assembly. They would be expected to line up outside the staff room to await their fate. Often, the bills would take considerable time to work their way through the system and it could come as a complete surprise to the billee to hear his name announced. It would only be when the sentence was about to be delivered that they would be reminded. Some teachers would eschew the formality of the bill system and would take the law into their own hands, whacking kids on the spot. Some had their own gym shoes, specially adapted for the purpose of flagellating the bums of kids who had been talking in line, or whatever. Most of the teachers seemed to dislike this aspect of their work and did it with a heavy heart. A minority didn't seem to mind it at all. A few seemed to see a religious significance in suffering physically for the expiation of sinful behaviour. I was last 'strapped' when I was sixteen because I would not bring in any kit for their stupid games, preferring to read uplifting works of literature in the library. 'If you don't bring in kit, Jones, you stand at the edge of the pitch and watch the other boys play. Put your hands out'. The following year I was the chair of the Liverpool section of the National Union of School Students. Banning corporal punishment was one of our main campaigning issues

The end of the school day was the time for settling scores. This usually took place in the woods opposite the school or by the water tower. St Kevs was no place for cissies to be sure. But if, like me, you wanted nothing to do with scrapping it wasn't hard to avoid. You just had to know your way around and who to avoid eye contact with. As in other schools we operated a 'cock' system. The primary schools had their own cocks, naturally. But when the move came to senior school these positions had to be renegotiated among a much larger population. This sorted out the blaggers who had only been cocks of their primary schools through bluff and bluster. By the time it came to St Kev's order had to be reestablished. As I recall, each year had its own cock. Then there was an overall school cock; the cock of cocks. To the best of my recollection, there were no 'house cocks'. That public school style esprit de corps could not be generated for the houses, no matter how hard the teachers tried to promote it. The only cocks whose names I can remember were the brothers Tony and Malcolm Cheong, two boys of Chinese descent. Who knows how or why two of the tiny number of boys in the school from a minority ethnic group came to be so good at fighting?

I was at the other end of the school spectrum from all this fighting. I fancied myself as an intellectual and an aesthete. And the school was that big, it was possible to avoid all that nonsense if you didn't mind occasionally swallowing a bit of pride.I think that I only ever had one fight during my school years and that was with one of my best mates, the gambling supremo and that was nothing to do with school. But some of my schoolmates were prominent in the cock play offs. Two of the lads in my class were contenders. Another lad, took part in fights too, although passively. He seemed to attract the attention of the ugly brute division of the scrappers. I reckon they were enraged by his David Cassidy style good looks and popularity with girls. One of them, a particularly dismal specimen, took a chair to his front teeth at a Parent Teacher Association event in an entirely unprovoked attack that took place without the benefit of any build up. I saw the miscreant a few years ago, a burnt out wreck of a man. To be honest, I didn't feel much sympathy.

In the end it was the ageing of the Kirkby population and the wilful flouting of the Pope's advice on contraception which did for Saint Kevins. The boys were not coming forward in their previous droves and by the 1980s the church was hard up for cash and found it almost impossible to fend off the lustful advances of property developers, keen to turn our pioneering school into a housing estate. It was the Pope versus mammon, and mammon won.

In a Catholic Style

"King in a Catholic Style". Song by China Crisis, St Kevins boys.

Strange as it might sound, considering my later ideological position, I have no regrets about going to a Catholic school, apart from the fact that it was single sex, obviously. The indoctrination into Catholic thinking has helped me see the world through another lens throughout my whole life, even if I find that lens distorting and reliably inaccurate. When I was at university there was a craze for reading the short stories of Frank O'Connor, the Irish writer. Myself and an Irish friend spent three months answering such questions as 'What is a bad confession?'. To have an in depth acquaintance with religion is like having a foreign language; you can think in a different way and express your thoughts in a different code. On a recent visit to Poland I put my head into a church. I saw people genuflecting, crossing themselves and using the holy water, which few of my secular contemporaries would understand. I still get a tickle in the hairs of my neck if I hear 'Faith Of Our Fathers' and would vote for it's tune (just the tune!) to become the next national anthem, if we were ever given the choice. It would certainly beat the current dirge. It has the uplifting quality of the 'Marseillaise', without the whole, you know, guillotine thing. Mind you, to be non sectarian for a moment, I think the same about 'The Sash My Father Wore', for a great marching tune.

When my parents first enrolled me in St Maries RC infant school they were both red hot religionists from families who had pictures of Jesus exposing his flaming, bare heart on their walls. In our house there was a blue statue of the Virgin Mary. I have a very early memory of being hawked out of church in the Dingle, close to where my Nan lived, for persistent crying. My dad Billy especially took his religion seriously, he didn't do things by halves. Perhaps this all or nothing approach is what made him eventually change his views. He became active in the joiners union, the Amalgamated Society of Woodworkers (ASW). This brought him into contact with men he had heard denounced from the pulpit. Notable among these was one Leo McGree but there were others: Joe Leith, Frank Marsh and many others. These were the sort of extremists who demanded toilets on building sites, helmets for building workers and the right not to work in the rain without protective clothes. Billy both liked and admired these men but because they were communists he had heard them denounced at election time and heard warnings that anyone voting for them would be defying the church. It didn't take long before my dad started to entertain doubts. His doubts extended beyond his union work and entered social policy. He reasoned, 'If the church is against contraception, how come the Catholic families in Kirkby were so small?' I think that this latter question was crucial in his thinking. If he could defy the church on such a crucial question in his own personal life, what was the basis of the rest of his beliefs? So he stopped going to church and started to change his attitude to the priests who came on weekly domestic calls. Years later, became a member of the Communist Party of Great Britain and became a prominent union activist on Merseyside. He won a lifetime service award from his union when he retired. He also won the Robert Noonan prize for services to the labour movement. As I say, he didn't do things by halves. He was the chair of the committee set up to defend the men sent to prison after the building workers strike in 1972, one of whom was Ricky Tomlinson.

So for me it was the New Testament at school and the Daily Worker at home. The question of taking me out of the school never arose. I was happy at school and I was in a stable group of mates and doing well. Why move? And, fair play to the school, the question of moving was never raised by the Catholic authorities, though they must have known about dad. Only one teacher even broached the subject. This was some idiot who sat me down and indicated that he knew about Billy's beliefs and indicated that his activities might damage my own career ambitions. Little did he know! The North West TUC obtained a leaked copy of blacklist information obtained from the shadowy and sinister Economic League which listed my entire family as subversives.

In any case, until I was fourteen I was an enthusiastic Catholic school boy. I wasn't quite as enthusiastic as many of my mates who were altar boys, to be sure. And I certainly wasn't as enthusiastic as the boys who self-selected for a life of celibacy by volunteering to go to a seminary and train as a priest. There were two lads who disappeared from our ranks to go down this route. One went down south and one went to a seminary in Ormskirk. Their recruitment, or rather their recognition of a 'calling' as it would have been expressed, must have been seen by many in the school hierarchy as a peak achievement. The priesthood still held a lot of sway at the schools. I distinctly remember in the infants, at the age of six or seven, having the senior local priest coming into the class and after introductions saying 'Now children I want to tell you something very important. You should not be afraid of dying'. Blimey! The thought hadn't even occurred to me before that. I was more concerned about who among my lad friends could wee highest up the toilet wall. It was Tony D____ by the way. But dying? Way to give us nightmares, Father.

These were heady times in the church. Vatican II had got rid of the Latin mass and the church attempted to make itself more relevant to the modern era. We heard lots and lots about Vatican II. Looking back, I wonder if there weren't arguments in the staff room about all of this. After all, many people valued the timeless, unchanging character of Catholicism above all else. What did they make of this new, guitar strumming, Kumbayar singing church? Were there ideological daggers drawn in the staff rooms? Who knows?

But by fourteen years of age the wheels were starting to come off my Catholicism along with other lads in class. By fourteen, any teacher who was prepared to go into bat would have to face our remorseless schoolboy logic. As though we had thought up the objections for the first time we would bait them with: 'So Sir, you claim that an all powerful, all seeing and all benevolent God exists. Yet there is Nazism earthquakes and starvation. Take your pick, which of those claims would you like to drop?'. The secular teachers would not get engaged but the believers were always game for this sort of challenge. We thought it was a wheeze to get out of talking about quadratic equations or Latin declensions. But in fact these arguments in class served an invaluable purpose. They sharpened our minds about the nature of philosophical debate and introduced us to subjects in religion which have rattled down the centuries. In our class, three went on to study philosophy at university. This cannot be a coincidence.

The lads who had followed their calling to seminary, by fourteen were back among us. We were by this time hardened sceptics who took no religious precept on trust. Everything was up for grabs. That said, it is notable that of our group a large number went on to be highly respected figures in the Catholic education system on Merseyside. One, went on to be the adored head of one of the feeder schools to St Kevins. But many had careers which were just as notable. The church may not have recruited anyone to the celibacy from our group, but there were plenty of other services one of their old boys could render to the one, true, apostolic church.

We did a lot of praying in school. Start of assembly, end of assembly. Start of class, end of class (for the religious teachers). Before dinner, after dinner. Then there were the micro acts of religion. In all our exercise books we were supposed to write in the top corner AMDG. This stood for: Ad Majorem Dei Gloriam, to the greater glory of God. I did not know that it meant this at the time, but who cared? The effort was minimal and, if it kept you from the attentions of The Man, why would you not? By

1966 the church had abandoned the Latin mass, apart from some nutcase hold outs in France who risked the loss of their immortal souls by defying the Pope. I can vaguely remember the mass being said in Latin and phrases still come back to me unbidden: Et cum spiritu tuo for instance. The 'academic' streams were still taught Latin, even though the mass was now in English. We were told that Latin helps you to understand other European languages. We were told that you needed Latin to be a doctor. We were told that Latin helped you to think logically. But I reckon that the teaching of Latin was a hangover from the Latin mass era, and teaching it to us was in hopes that we might become priests already adept at the lingo.

There were a few priests and nuns who came to teach us. Most of these were Irish. I remember one of them clearly, though my visual recollection of him gets confused with Father Dougal in the sitcom Father Ted. This was Father 'Pop' Hughes. I can't even remember what he was supposed to be teaching us, but you could always get him onto the subject of the Theatre of the Absurd and writers such as Beckett, Pinter and so on. He would come alive at their insistence that beyond a certain point, language lost its ability to contain anything meaningful in the way of communication. This was a very interesting perspective and was the sort of idea that had never occurred to me. Interesting lessons, nice man. And the odd thing was, he was considerably less formal and dogmatic than many of his colleagues who had not received the Call. One time we were forced to watch an anti drugs film in class which inevitably ended with the young girl who had left the path of righteousness being cremated. As the coffin was disappearing beyond the crematorium curtains Pop Hughes said in a stage whisper 'Thunderbirds Are Go!'

Pop Hughes was that sort of educational optimist who is confident that decent subjects enthusiastically delivered will hit home. He was enthusiastic about the Catholic philosopher Teilhard de Chardin and other church modernists even though he was a controversial figure in the church. He would smilingly welcome us attempting to overturn his faith. I wonder what happened to him.

Not all teachers were this informal. There was one who used to describe, in the sort of blistering, agonising detail that would today come with a parental guidance sticker, the suffering of Christ in his passion. I always thought that 'passion' was a strange word to choose for torture and murder, but what am I, a theologian? He would discuss the exact type of middle eastern bush that would furnish the thorns for Christ's mocking crown. These weren't your bramble or rose thorns, oh no. These were full on, massive thorns. And do you think his crown was placed gently on his head? No way. It was rammed on by the cursing Roman soldiery. Turning to the nails, they couldn't possibly have gone through his hands. They would have torn through the flesh and he would have fallen off the cross. And say what you like about the Romans, they would never have allowed that. They were engineers. No, the nails would have gone between the radius and ulnar bones for the extra purchase this would give them. On and on and on like this. Blood, pain, violence and death, on and on. It seemed odd then, it seems odd now.

But, as I say, I didn't regret any of my Catholic education though by the age of fifteen I was an active member of the Young Communist League. I was of that faction in the League that favoured 'Christian Marxist Dialogue', an attempt to emphasise the ideas that Christians and

Communists had in common rather than those which divided us.

This is how I came to terms with my Catholic education. There was no shortage of discussion about 'Liberation Theology' either so it wasnt difficult to find a bridge to our teachers, however hostile I was to the rest of it.

The Teachers

'Wake up at the back there!' Catchphrase, Jimmy Edwards as 'Whack-O'

I can imagine that in middle class dinner parties in the 1960s the news that one of the diners had applied to teach in a huge comprehensive in Kirkby would have raised an incredulous eyebrow or two. But Why? Are you mad? The place had a reputation. It was on the telly for its reputation. It was in black and white. So I suspect that among the staff there were genuine idealists, people who had a missionary zeal to bring education to the culture of under achievement that was proletarian Kirkby. You could sense it too, in class. There was a buzz in class when you had a liberation theology, left leaning teacher. There was a feeling in the room that there was a sympatico at the blackboard. Not a walkover but not a cynic either. Obviously there were exceptions to this rule. There was one whopper who had taken it upon himself to police the corridors outside his classroom, a one man vigilante squad. He would collect boys who had infringed one of his arbitrary rules and would impose his own regime of sanctions. 'Making the punishment fit the crime' he was fond of saying, in a cack-handed tribute to Gilbert and Sullivan. When we were about fifteen we were all in his class one day and he dragged some wretch in from the corridor. The boy was scared and was not putting his hand out to receive his flagellation. So Mr Thwackum said 'If you don't put your hand out I'll get these boys (pointing at us) to hold you down'. Good luck with that, Sir. I reckon not one of us would have raised a hand. We would have all gone conscientious objector on him.

But these were the few exceptions, and I'm glad they are out of the way because now we can get on to the inspirers.

Starting from the top, the headmaster. There was only one headmaster in all the time that I was there and that was Mr Frank 'Charlie' Moorhead. He was an MA (Cantab) subject unknown and he did not have a local accent. A Google search which enters his name brings nothing up which is surprising, considering his standing in the community. I didn't like him, but I have come to admire him. He was a somewhat distant figure, as is to be expected in a school containing so many staff and he ran the place with theocratic fervour. But...he always had a nice word about the local population, in public anyway. He was particularly gushing about the mothers of Kirkby who, he argued, were the glue that held the whole show together. Correct, Mr M. He also aimed for high standards from the kids. If by high you mean that he wanted St Kevs to be the sort of place that posh people would wish to send their kids to. He aimed for a sort of public school ethos, with a Latin motto and everything: 'Respice Finem', Look To The End. Again, the uncomfortable focus on dying that was started with Father Doom in the infants. It is odd now to recall the degree to which Charlie pushed his public school vision. Twice weekly we had a collective, half school assembly that he would harangue. The school was just too big for a whole school get-together to be held, ever. When everyone was quiet in would sweep Charlie in an academic gown, like a refugee from 'Goodbye Mr Chips'. Kids would hum, undetected, the theme tune from the TV series Batman, which was then all the rage.

When he was settled on stage we would then be given a religiously themed address. One of his secular specialities was in the persecution of bullies. If any bullying had been detected on his manor he would promise us, faithfully promise us, that the guilty party would be detected and punished by the end of the day. The boys responsible would be invited to own up to their crimes with the promise that it would go much worse for them if they had to be winkled out. This always struck me as a good deal, a sort of Kirkby plea bargain if you will. If there was no result from this carrot, out would come the stick. Charlie would send out his marshals to investigate.

His Grace Archbishop Beck congratulates St. Kevin's head boy, Christopher Jones, watched by headmaster Mr. Frank Moorhead and chairman of the governors Mr. Eddie Aylward (left). (AE1541)

Me, the scruff, shaking the hand of Archbishop Beck, with Charlie Moorhead looking on.

I remember one teacher, named for some reason after

55

the cartoon character Elmer Fudd, coming into our class after one outrage and asking if any of us knew the identity of someone called 'Fraz'. No sir, but I do know a Macca, is that any good?

One of the things I admired about Charlie was that he retained his vision, despite everything, of the dreaming spires of St Kevins nestled on the banks of the river Alt. Against the daily evidence of his own eyes, for instance the boys smoking outside the shops and in sight of his office , I think in his mind he clung to a vision of us 'talking posh' in boaters. A little slice of Brideshead that landed in the area of our Urban District Council. It was perhaps to disturb this vision that me and a couple of mates decided to paint, in letters two feet high and directly opposite his office the slogan 'Peace Through Socialism' on the wall of the chippy. Take that with your morning coffee, Charlie! Only things didn't go exactly to plan. Nerves rather got the better of me and in my hurry to get the job done I misspelt the word 'through' as 'throgh' and I only realised my mistake when I had finished the slogan and stood back to read it. Hurriedly I had to try to rectify my mistake by inserting the missing U. But it ended up looking like 'thro^{u}gh'. I felt that I had let down the international labour movement and for the rest of my school career, looking at it made me cringe. I am not sure, either, what would have bothered Mr Moorhead most if he knew one of his boys was behind this wanton vandalism; the politics or the grammar.

And talking posh was no idle ambition for Charlie as I shall reveal. By the time we were in sixth form we were organised among ourselves. We had our own committee. We had fund raising activities. We donated to the coffers of the National Union of School Students and in my final year the lads elected me, a known member of the Young Communist League, to be head boy. A representative group of us were invited over to Charlie's office periodically for a pep talk. All the rebels used to go. One was a fellow traveller of mine, both politically and academically. Good at French too. There was a proto anarchist. Another was always good for a hilarious thumbnail sketch of the proceedings after the event and a few other boys. At one meeting he asked what we were timetabled for after our meeting. 'What?' I asked, 'Subjectwise?'. This did not go down well. He turned to his deputy and said in an exasperated voice 'Don't you hate the way these Americanisms have crept into British English, Mr Whatsisname?' Perhaps I should have apologised in my poshest voice: 'Parding Mr Moorhead'. He also used to regale us with stories from his own varsity years in the 1930s when he and his mates would break up Communist Party meetings. It was hard to avoid the conclusion that these remarks were a little pointed. One time he told us that he had heard some very disturbing news. He had been told that there were some boys who were 'agin' the government. Outside of the Beverly Hillbillies I had never heard anyone use the word 'agin'. We shook our heads in disbelief.

Many years later a member of staff who shared a church with my mother in law told her that the fact that we argued back at Charlie in his own office became the talk of the school's staff rooms. Rebellion was as welcome in Saint Kevs as it was in Franco's Spain, be it from the kids or the staff. It was warming to think that our polite and restrained effort at subversion were recognised by the NUT members.

Below Mr Moorhead were the rest of the staff. One in the hierarchy immediately below Charlie was Mr 'Bob'

Hope, our house master. I have only just realised that the name 'Bob' was given to him in honour of the American comedy superstar of that ilk: Bob Hope. Mr 'Hopey' Hope was a member of the school PE staff. There were persistent but unsubstantiated claims that in a previous career he had been a ballet dancer. It is hard to know whether this would be likely. Certainly he had the physique. But he was also a 'man's man', as far from the stereotype of the effete ballet dancer as you could imagine. It wouldn't have surprised me though. Hopey was a very humane sort of man and one that was easily approached. It was his responsibility to administer the strappings that had been sent to him as bills. But when he was getting ready to wallop a boy (and we were all particularly fearful of being walloped by him given the size of his arms) his head would develop an odd sort of tremor that I put down to rage at the time. Looking back, I suspect that this was not the sort of job he enjoyed as part of his role. The tremor was probably the result of him being a bit messed up by the whole thing. Everyone liked Hopey. Nobody wanted to get strapped by him.

I am ashamed to say that many of the teachers I liked, I have no firm memories of. Mr Malone (English), 'Dermy'

Glennon (English), Mr Carter (French) I had a lot of affection and respect for them all, but I cant bring any events to mind. Mr Cunningham 'Sly Bacon' I also liked, and can remember his withering classroom wit. One kid didn't bring any of his textbooks to class. He did not know whether we would be reading book A or book B, was his excuse. 'I see' said Mr C 'You thought that you didn't know which book to bring in, so you played safe and didn't bring any'. One of the members of the geography staff, a large man in late middle age, claimed to be able to hypnotise people and would put a boy into a trance as a sort of party trick at the end of a class, or in those end of term days when you could bring games in. I never saw it myself, and frankly I didnt believe it. Any St Kevs kid worth his salt would have known what a 'hypnotised boy' routine looked like and would have played the part for laughs. You would have a hard time explaining in class hypnotism to an Ofsted inspector these days.

There were other teachers I recall because of some eccentricity. One was a maths teacher called Mr Shaw. Under his ginger moustache he had somewhat protruding teeth which, in a minor way, affected his speech. So far so unremarkable. But he also had one of those shapeless Essex type southern accents which rendered everything he said in anger hilarious. If the lads were talking during class he would lose it and shriek 'Shaddap, or you git aht!'. I still say this to my kids if they start mocking me. I think they find it hard to understand why I laugh every time I utter these words.

One of the few pre A level teachers I can attach any memories to is 'Vinny' Kelly, the Latin teacher. A quiet and unassuming man, he took us on a school trip to the Roman ruins of the west country and south Wales, and taking in Bath, Salisbury and Stonehenge. We would pile into a van and drive from site to site, staying in youth hostels. We also visited Bristol, and I was so impressed by the place that I went to live there after university. In that sense the trip with Vinny was life changing. In one of the youth hostels we had to share a dorm with kids from somewhere called Latymer High, a genuinely posh school. One of our number made sleep almost impossible by gently mocking them late into the night. I don't know what they made of it all, but we thought it was hilarious.

At the ruins Vinny would translate the Latin inscriptions for us and would fill in the background details of the layout of Roman buildings. It was a lovely trip and Vinny was a genial and well tempered guide. We went to Tintern Abbey and while we were there we met some American tourists and got chatting to them. The woman of the couple said to the man in a New York accent 'Gee, don't they talk like the Beatles!' which we took as an entirely undeserved compliment.

For the rest of the teachers, the most that I remember are the ones who took us for A levels. The classes were smaller so it is easier to recall their quirks and eccentricities. We were closer up. I took French (the only subject at school I felt I was any good at), history and English. Hardly anybody fancied French and it was touch and go for a while whether we would be able to do it to A level. In the end they found a teacher for the three of us. The teacher was Mr 'Monty' Edwards. He was a nice, older, posh gentleman whose eyebrows curled up at the end which earned him the alternate sobriquet of 'Lucifer'. He was a good linguist all right and had clearly been a university man himself in his youth. French was not his only language either. I used to get him to translate the titles of songs by the band Santana, which all my mates were listening to at the time. But I reckon that the light had gone out in his enthusiasm for teaching modern languages. By the time he came to us he was much more at home talking about his favourite subject: spiritualism. At the end of our year with him we would have struggled to comment on the set texts for the course: Francois Mauriac, Moliere and Anatole France. We could have sat an exam on ectoplasm though, and could have had a go at an essay entitled 'Spiritualism is consistent with the core beliefs of Roman Catholicism - Discuss'. He laid great emphasis on those bits of the New Testament which talked about being 'born again'. He seemed to think that this gave scriptural bulk to his arguments about reincarnation. We didn't mind though. Table tapping was, in fact, infinitely more interesting than French Catholic misery guts Mauriac any day of the week. The pigeons came home to roost in the second year though when we realised how far we had fallen behind on the syllabus.

I met Monty many years later, perhaps thirty odd. I was walking the streets in the area I now live in, Aigburth. There he was, mowing his lawn in the sunshine. I recognised him immediately although I am not sure he recognised me. At school he seemed as ancient as hell, think Godfrey in Dad's Army, but here he looked no older than back then. I introduced myself to him and said thank you for all his efforts, leaving aside the question of his lunatic commitment to spiritualism. I felt he deserved a pat on the back. He is no longer at the address and I wonder if he hasn't packed up his ectoplasm and shuffled off to his next incarnation.

Replacing him in the second year of A level was Miss Eccleshall. She was a local girl, of about twenty five I would guess. She lived in a maisonette on the East Lancashire Road close to Townsend Avenue, so not posh. I know this because I saw her getting off the bus there once. She was a graduate of Lancaster University (I think), but that is practically all I know of her personal history. I don't even know where she went for her year in France. She didn't strike me as a particularly private person, it's just that she felt that there was a lot of ground to travel to make up for the time we had spent 'between worlds' with Monty. She was sharp, business like, funny and professional. The only idea she gave us of her irritation about year one was an intake of breath and a thinning of the lips when we declared our ignorance of stuff we should have known about. Nothing was actually said. A true professional. I wonder what happened to her.

A group of teachers I do remember were the French assistants. The lads in our class regarded them as fair and square military targets. We were mean to those students, whose grasp of English was frequently incomplete. The boys would say all sorts of things to and about them using freshly minted slang words in our harsh accents and they had no idea what we were saying. What they could understand was the noise level which was frequently intense. Their classroom control was inevitably sketchy and they often looked as though they were struggling with the urge to run away. It got too much for one of them, Monsieur Rafatin (I'm spelling from the sound of his name). He was a sharply dressed individual who always taught in a fitted blazer and had a beard like George the fifth. He came from Perpignan and amused us with tales of his stone throwing activities during the student rebellion in the late 1960s. To moi, fascinating. Anyway, one day the student rebellion he had in his own class became too much for him and he must have decided that desperate measures had to be taken with someone 'pour encourager les autres'. He picked out one lad who was made to go up to the front of the class. We, and he, expected a verbal rebuke, tops. In fact M. Rafatin made Bernie stand in front of him while he slapped his face one way, then smack with his back hand the other way. It couldn't have been more dramatic if he had challenged Bernie to a duel. Now that's what I call a French lesson.

Another assistant I recall was Monsieur Patrique Gatinet. He was from Brittany and represented the sort of teacher who I wanted to be like as a man. He was informal, friendly and bright with excellent English. By the time we met him one of the three lads who took French had left school. This was doubly disappointing because he would have had academic success had he stayed on, I am sure of it. So that left two of us doing French. Patrique invited us to a party in his flat just off Lark Lane. His flat was situated two doors up from a flat I spent ten years in later in life. I also went with him to see the Costa Gavros film Z about the Greek Colonels coup in Greece. This was played to a packed house at the university and excited some emotion because the crack down in Greece was still a recent event.

The other assistant, or rather assistante, that I remember was altogether of a different order. Imagine the scene in Kirkby. An absence of sun and an excess of rain and a diet of chips, egg and beans meant that everyone in the town was to one degree or another…pasty, there is no other word for it. Add to that, the fashion that most appealed to the greater part of the girls of Kirkby at that time was a female imitation of the bovver boy get up. They wore brown 'Crombie' style suits with a fake handkerchief sticking out of a top pocket and a haircut which was as close as a girl could go to the chrome dome pates of the boy skinheads. So, pasty girls in masculinised clothes and big, clumpy, boot style shoes. Are you getting the picture?

Into this descended a young woman who might as well have been Brigitte Bardot. Tanned, with hair tumbling across every perfectly formed surface it touched, she was 'lovely of face, and perfect in the attributes of grace'. Mademoiselle Nicole caused us all to stand still and stare. I am not sure I knew that women like her existed. A hush followed her through the corridors. The glamour of the French Riviera, she seemed to be from a different world. And we didn't have her, not even for one lesson. Such is the unfairness of life, the 'natural cussedness of things'. We were probably being punished for something we had done in a previous life, as Monty would have said. Tant Pis!

The other group of A level teachers who took us were those from the history department. Mr 'Arsey Thomo' Thompson took us through European history 1870-1939 and Mr Moynihan took us for British historical documents. Both teachers were very nice men though they were at opposite ends of the pedagogical spectrum. Thomo was slow speaking and thoughtful. His lessons consisted in reading through what appeared to be his handwritten notes from university. He probably wrote them up the night before the lessons, but they looked like ancient parchments to us. For that reason his lessons could be a bit of a slog unless we could liven things up by challenging some of his basic assumptions. He dragged us through the causes of the first world war right enough, pointing out all of the landmarks that were in our textbooks. But if one of us challenged him: 'Hang on Sir. Wasn't the first world war all about the rivalries of competing empires, driven by elites which sent working class young men in their thousands to their deaths in a war they had no material interest in fighting?', the strangest thing would happen. He would stop his reading and stare into space. For ages. It was as though the thought had never occurred to him until that very moment. We didn't exactly time these trances, but you get the idea. We were aware of them. And fair play to him, he would frequently come back with a reasoned point of view that often met us half way, if there was anything in our question. Thomo was a nice man. He had also been our teacher in our pre A level years when we were about fifteen. He gave us the job of picking a project to investigate ourselves, independently. Unsurprisingly, I chose the origins of the trade union movement. This obviously appealed to him, because one day he kept me back in class and gave me a published diary of a mill worker in the mid 19th century. The worker in question nearly starved to death during one of the periodic slumps in the cotton industry. The man was also 'strong in the union'. I have tried to find this document many times since, with no luck. But the way that Arsey saw my enthusiasm and fed it with contributions of his own made me think that the man had depths that were not obvious at first sight. And so I always warmed to him and his eccentric teaching style only served to endear him to me.

Our other teacher for history was Mr 'Tom' Moynihan. He had the hairiest ears I had ever seen, huge sproutings of jet black hair that were entirely undisciplined. He also had a serious smoking habit and would measure the length of his classes by how needful were his lungs for a fag. 'Well boys, my lungs are informing me that we are approaching break time....' Whereas we used to try to alarm Arsey with unfamiliar ideas, in Mr Moynihan's class it was the other way around. He taught us how to write an essay about contemporary historical documents. His lessons are still front and centre of my approach to reading documents today. Who is telling me this? When was this document produced? Are they an eye witness, or did someone tell them about these matters? Does the writer of this document have any conflicts of interest with the truth? Have they got their mind on subsequent biographies? His classes led you to challenge some of your own basic assumptions. I can only imagine his chagrin when one boy, when asked how he knew some claim that he was spouting was true, said 'It was in the paper'. He must have felt that two years worth of training in document scepticism was wasted.

Mr Moynihan had gone to university in St Andrews in Scotland and when he started speaking on the subject it was obvious that a part of him had never left. He spoke with such affection about the place that he gave the impression that he thought that, after university, life had gone a bit downhill. When I came to apply for university he gave me some top class advice. I had to choose between University College of North Wales in Bangor and Sheffield University. I was edging towards Sheffield. But Mr M argued that, at 18, I should be going for the greatest breadth of experience. I had been brought up, he said, in a northern industrial town, why go to another? He said that it was highly unlikely that I would ever get the chance to live in the heart of Welsh speaking Wales ever again and I should grab it. 'If the choice was between UCNW and the Sorbonne, I'd say go to the Sorbonne. But Sheffield?' I took his advice and never regretted it.

In one of his lessons he told us that an ex pupil had applied to join the intelligence services and that he himself had been interviewed by spooks as part of the positive vetting process. In the course of the interview he said that they let slip some aspects of his university life which indicated that they knew more about him than he was entirely comfortable with. I didn't get the impression that he was an over enthusiastic religionist, though I could be wrong about that. When we presented him with our familiar schoolboy litany of doubts about the Catholic church he would always encourage us to look beyond what he called the 'accretions' which had attached to the church over the centuries. He argued that in considering religion, we ought to look to the origins and the character of Jesus for inspiration, leaving aside the apparatus of the bureaucratic superstructures that had been constructed over 2000 years.

The other big influence on my life came from the art department and its allies. St Kevins had a number of after hours clubs and I joined many of them. But by the age of 15 or 16 I started to attend the Art Club with my friends. This was not really part of the main art department and I can only imagine the staff room eyebrows it must have raised. It was run by two teachers Bob Williams and Paddy Adamson. To the best of my recall these were recent graduates from the Liverpool School of Art, on Hope Street. This was a progressive and well regarded establishment at a time when Liverpool was still riding high in the art world. Liverpool poets, playwrights and musicians were setting the pace. The Liverpool Poets had just been published by Adrien Henri, Roger McGough and Brian Patten while the Everyman Theatre down the road from the art college was establishing a groundbreaking reputation. It was from the artistic and rebellious cauldron that Bob and Paddy emerged. To describe them as unconventional would be to understate the case. Long haired, irreverent and dressed oddly, for Kirkby anyway, they stood out in what was still a very conformist school. Bob would show up for school in a Triumph TR7 open topped sports car. Paddy was the boys favourite because apart from anything else, he wasn't that much older than us. 22? 23?

But it was to be Bob whose influence on my life was to be the most transformative. Whether it was in literature, art, cinema, theatre or lifestyle after Bob, nothing was the same. He would drive us around in his car, take us to events, introduce us to friends and colleagues and lend us his various flats if he went away for the weekend. He let us stay in his girlfriend's flat on Gambier Terrace once. She had a samurai suit of armour. She was, I think, a lecturer at the college and she had a fancy stereo. The sound of Plum Blossom by Yusuf Lateef brings back that weekend as does the cover of Bringing it all Back Home, which I took to be us, in that flat. Bob showed us a style of life that was far from the one we had grown into and once I got a taste of it, there was no going back. He introduced us to Jack Kerouac, to William Burroughs, to the Beatles White Album (hot off the presses), to John Keats and to the John Moores art biennials in the Walker Art Gallery. He introduced us to people too. His friend Jean was an actress in the Everyman. She lived in Geneva Road in Kensington. At the same time Bob listened a lot to a vinyl record he had of The Marat Sade. This was a play about a theatre production staged by inmates of an insane asylum in post revolutionary France. The imagined production concerned the assassination of Jean Paul Marat by Charlotte Corday and had been written by the Marquis de Sade. In Britain the play was performed by the Royal Shakespeare Company and was produced by Peter Brook. I have a suspicion that his friend Jean appeared in the Marat Sade and that she was Jeanette Landis, possibly appearing in a play in Liverpool. It looked like her anyway.

The Marquis de Sade got Bob into a heap of trouble in school. Bob was reading the 101 nights of Sodom by de Sade, one of the most disturbing and obscene books ever written. My friend, the king of the gambling fraternity, 'borrowed' the book from Bob's briefcase and when his dad saw the book he hit the roof and took it to show Charlie Moorhead who also hit the roof. I don't know how Bob recovered from that fiasco, but after it his days at the school were numbered. I think Charlie put it to Bob that there was no future for him at St Kevs, so eventually he left. He teamed up with a local builder and in partnership with the head of economics he founded a damp coursing firm, of all things. How are the mighty fallen! I won't give the name of the firm in case anyone has still got one of Bob's guarantees of workmanship. Bob went from this business into redeveloping the Pearl Insurance building by Lime Street Station as Rockfords, a 'nite spot'.

Paddy was a nice bloke too, but his hang out was the pottery department. I avoided pottery, I didn't like the dry feeling clay gave my hands. I'm sensitive like that. He kind of disappeared from school in an inexplicable way. The next I heard of him was when I was in the first year of university when it was reported on the news in April that the body of a Mr Patrick Adamson had been found on the mountains. He had been missing since the previous Autumn. Poor Paddy. I went on a camping trip to Devon with Paddy and Bob and a few other lads in 1968. I know it was that date because, after a brief trip away to see a girlfriend in Bristol, Paddy came back with the news of an assassination attempt that had been made on the life of Andy Warhol in New York.

One of Bob and Paddys friends inside the school was a French teacher called Pauline Hughes. In my memory I always confuse her look with that of the folk singer Sandy Denny. She started a film society in the school, so naturally, I was up for that. I only recall one film that we saw which was 'Some Like It Hot'. With the plot resting on heavy layers of sexuality courtesy of Marilyn Munroe, I wonder if Charlie had OK'd the event or if this was the reason that film club withered on the vine. But the upshot of the event was that we got to know Miss Hughes. She had a brother at the school. He was a bull necked rugby type in the PE department but she was all arts, music and sophistication. She had a flat in one of the tower blocks opposite our school and she invited me and my other mates from Art Club for tea one night. That's tea, not dinner and definitely not supper. I think it was the first time that I had ever tasted that long spaghetti that came in blue packets. You don't seem to see them any more. Anyway, after tea, she let us loose on her record collection. I had brought a reel to reel tape recorder I'd got for a birthday. I recorded 'White Light, White Heat' by Velvet Underground. Also A Saucerful of Secrets by Pink Floyd and the album Santana. Those records must have been just off the boat and there was us listening away, in Kirkby. It was a windy night and I was recording with a microphone, so when I hear any of those records I still hear the sound of the wind in the background.

Jaundiced souls have suggested that Bob's encouragement of his young companions might not have been as innocent as it seemed. Those were different times, and we were not as alive as we are now to the possibility that school kids can be taken advantage of. But if there was any untoward interest in us, there was little to suggest it from his behaviour. He didn't ever do anything to me, not so much as a hug. In fact, in that way, he was rather stand offish if anything.

The same could not be said about some of the more respectable members of St Kevs staff. There was one who had created a curious modification to the corporal punishment policy of the school. Getting a question wrong in class could mean that you were called to the front of the class and walloped, bare handed, on the bum. That wasn't all. The hand would linger longingly over our peachy arses and would cop a lengthy feel. It was such a well known thing he did, that me and a mate used to play up to it. While the lads would watch and try, often unsuccessfully to control their laughter, we would camp it up with him groping away in full view of the class. It always struck me as incredible that even years later, we could have got the idiot sent to prison for his indiscretion.

The only legally questionable thing we ever saw Bob get up to was rolling up a joint. Not that I ever had any, but even this I took as an essential part of my pre university education.

We were regularly put in front of student teachers. I used to feel very sorry for these fresh faced lambs sent to the slaughter. They would try perfectly planned lessons on us, but would meet with a wall of sullen non co-operation that rapidly degenerated into open mockery and rebellion. It was woeful to watch. The more that the teacher lost control, the better we considered things were going. The only time they achieved our cooperation was when some assessor came to sit at the back of the class with a clipboard. Even though we had little idea of why they were there we could sense that they (the assessor) was there to assess us (student teacher and boys). An unspoken solidarity would kick in which would mean that hands would go up to questions, silence would prevail and the student professor would indicate by facial expression that they thought we had been replaced by well mannered twins, all twenty five of us.

The Boys

"Then the whining schoolboy with his satchel and his shining morning face, creeping like a snail, unwillingly to school" William Shakespeare, As You Like It.

At upwards of 2000 boys St Kevins was one of the largest single sex schools in Europe but this was not the only remarkable fact about the school. The boys who attended it were almost entirely drawn from families who had been shifted out of the areas of Liverpool that were subject to the slum clearance schemes of the 1950s and 60s. In the main it was the clearance areas in the north of the city which filled Kirkby: Everton, Kirkdale, Scotland Road etc. Slum areas on the south of the city provided the population of Speke. Although Kirkby was officially in Lancashire, the population, and certainly the boys of St Kevins, regarded themselves as being Liverpool citizens. 100% Liverpool.

The lads in my school came from a watertight culture: this was a town of manual working class people. I did know some boys whose parents were teachers. There was one boy in my class whose dad, Mr Fitzsimmons, was a wildly popular teacher in our school, but he was an exception. Doubly exceptional was that Mr Fitz and his family lived on the estate, in Northwood. The thought that this was exceptional never occurred to me at the time. But for the most part the parents of the boys resembled the population of Liverpool: dockers, builders and manual workers in the factories of the industrial estate. In my class P1, the lads were clever, funny and well adapted to the world. Twelve of us are still very much in contact and we meet up on a regular basis. Nobody has changed fundamentally. I wonder if the other lads in the class meet up, if they do they don't invite us. The largest group ended up as school teachers, mostly in Catholic education. But there are civil servants, social housing administrators, motor industry workers and one from the fire service. I became a nurse, then a nurse teacher, then a university lecturer in nursing at Edge Hill University

Our school was also a monoculture in the racial profile of the boys. As a Catholic school there was a high incidence of people with an Irish background. But apart from the Irish priests there were very few Irish accents to be heard. The Irishness consisted in what my father in law called a 'fossilised' state. There were lots of Irish names on the register. Strangely, for an English school, shamrock was distributed on St Patrick's day and we would all know the words to the hymn 'Hail Glorious Saint Patrick Dear Saint of our Isle'. The isle in question here was not the Isle that England was on, obviously. There was explicit pride expressed in the sufferings of the English Catholic church and this was obvious from the names of the house halls; there was a high incidence of martyrs' names. But they were mainly English martyrs. Did the designers of the school wish to play down the overseas nature of UK Catholicism? Were they sensitive to the charge made by protestant sectarians that Catholics saw their religious loyalties as being located elsewhere, in Rome or Dublin? It is interesting to note that our other most favoured hymn, 'Faith of our Fathers' had an English as well as an Irish version and both wings of the Catholic population shared a pride in their resistance to protestant oppression. And by resistance, I mean death.

> Faith of our fathers, living still,
> In spite of dungeon, fire, and sword;
> Oh, how our hearts beat high with joy
> Whene'er we hear that glorious Word!

> Our fathers, chained in prisons dark,
> Were still in heart and conscience free;
> How sweet would be their children's fate,
> If they, like them, could die for thee!

The Welsh contribution to the school population was more muted. There were the Joneses and the Hughes, obviously. But the cultural stamp was not as visible. As for other racial stamps, they were barely measurable between the years 1966 and 1973. The boxer John Conteh was at our school, but he was older than me and I never knew him. There were the brothers Tony and Malcolm Cheong, both respective cocks of their years with Malcolm being the cock of cocks in the school. There was another boy, younger than me, who stood out. His name was Tony Magabe. He was a tall lad of African heritage who's name used to crop up with week by week regularity as being a champion field athlete because of his running speed. I think he played football too. He was also the cock of something or other, I forget. But in my memory he was also a popular boy, always surrounded by lads nine inches shorter than him.

But there were no Patels or Chouderys among either the boys or the staff. Did the religion of the school put South Asians off I wonder? Roughwood didn't seem to do any better attracting sub continentals. I don't recall any minority teachers on the staff either, apart from the Irish priests.

The only other minority boy I remember was a lad called Charlie Frost, an American boy. I never got to the bottom of what strange winds blew an American into our Kirkby sixth form, but there he was. I have always guessed that he had some sort of connection to the US air force base at Burtonwood, but this is mere speculation. He was tall, thin and had that sort of blond comb over wave that you can see in American youth films of the 1960s. One lad said that his hair wave was so pronounced that it made him sea sick to look at it. Charlie used to make us all jealous telling us how cheap records were in America. They used to swallow up any spare cash we had and the idea that they were almost given away in the USA was diabolical to us. Charlie also used to show up in decidedly non uniform trousers that had top to bottom multi coloured stripes. We were watching him go past the sixth form one day and one of the boys said 'He looks like a bar of rock.'

Let me be blunt. I think St Kevins was the funniest place I was ever in, and I have never laughed so much in my life. The funny wasn't always nice or respectable. It was frequently cruel especially if you were on the wrong end of it. But it was also achingly funny and I became very aware that the expression 'to die laughing' might not be an exaggeration in some cases. Sometimes, frequently, I could not breathe for laughing. Often, this was because the lads in class had said or done something intended to make you hoot. But sometimes it resulted from a random event that nobody could plan. We were queuing outside a class once and a boy, unknown to any of us, looked through the window on the door. Inside the class was a painfully thin female teacher winding up her class. Without looking at us, and apparently to himself, he said out loud in a Sigmund Freud style German accent: 'Iss the finest spider I have ever seen!' and just walked away without looking at the chaos he had caused in our queue with laughter. You had to be there I suppose.

As for sub cultures in the school, there were not many. We saw a bit of the early days of the skinhead craze with the boots, the cropped hair and the Crombie overcoats. Although the racism of the skinheads hadn't taken on the overtly political aspect it would later on in London, racism was pretty much the sea we swam in in the 70s. My dad used to wear a lapel badge depicting a black and a white hand shaking, and we followed the events of the US civil rights movement very closely at home. But outside the house it was pretty much bandit country for racism. I wonder how Tony Magabe managed it all. And the strange thing was, pretty much all the kids, skinheads and everyone, were devotees of Tamla Motown. I could never understand how they squared that circle in their heads.

Skinheads apart, there were the tiny minority of lads who saw themselves in the tradition of San Francisco and the hippies. It was music that they defined themselves by, so the music of the dance floor and of the charts was rejected and even despised. No, us sensitive souls preferred the Bob Dylans, The Simon and Garfunkles and the Carol Kings. Later on, in my case, Frank Zappa and the Mothers of Invention courtesy of John Bordo, a lad from my class. If you were a long haired hippy type there was always the threat that someone would give you a dig, but luckily, it never happened to me.

There was no drug culture that I was aware of anyway, apart from Bob rolling the odd joint in his car. These were the days of widespread, prescribed amphetamines too 'Mother's Little Helpers'. But as far as I knew, drug culture was London and New York not Tower Hill. And if there were drugs doing the rounds, nobody offered me any. It didn't even come up in conversation. We did get the odd dire warning from the staff, so we knew something was afoot. But not around here Sir.

There was a sprinkling of kids who were eccentrics. I used to walk to school with one lad, who seemed compelled to touch a certain number of surfaces on the way to school in a certain order. Why he did this or what his system was it never occurred to me to ask, but he lived on his own with his mum, and I guessed that there was something sad in his back story. Perhaps this was why I didn't like to pry. There was another kid whose life's ambition was to work on the buses and could therefore recall from heart the timetable of every bus that served Kirkby. And not just the council bus services either. Crosville, Ribble, you name it. If there was a bus that came into Kirkby, he knew its timetable.

Occasionally there would be kids who came in as 'blow ins' who would stay for a term and then disappear. In a school as big as ours we must have been exposed to some serious social problems even if they were all below the surface. Lots of kids were living with grandparents. Occasionally it would come out that someone's older sister was in reality their mum, that sort of thing. For a couple of terms there was a kid in our class who was incredibly posh. It was like having that kid in the Winslow Boy parachuted into the Bash Street school. It was never made clear why he was with us and he disappeared as quickly as he had arrived. I think some domestic drama had deprived him of his expectations as a pupil in a private school but hard facts were hard to come by in his case and then he was gone.

I am absolutely certain that bullying went on in Saint Kevins, but I don't think I saw that much. It depends what you call bullying I suppose. Some kids ended up on the wrong end of jokes more than others. An old friend of mine from my class said he thought I had been bullied, but honestly, I never saw it like that. But when it came to dinner money theft and physical violence, I didn't see much of that sort of thing. In a school that big I suppose you can mix in other circles. When it did happen, and if Charlie got wind of it he came down hard. Witnesses would be grilled. There would be collective punishments. Retribution would be severe when the guilty were brought to trial particularly if they hadn't come forward and confessed. But nobody I knew personally was ever convicted.

When it came to leaving school there were four options, five if you include the road to the priesthood that nobody took. Lots of kids just left, no job and no qualifications to show for their four years in full time education. Then there were the kids who joined the armed forces. One kid, a clever and personable lad whose name now escapes me, was trying to get into Sandhurst as I recall. I wonder if he managed it and if he did, how he managed the class prejudices of that institution in the early 1970s. A large number of boys got apprenticeships in every type of trade and, on serving their time, could be seen driving around in cars and wearing sharp clothes like the aristocracy of labour they were. Finally, there were the boys who 'stayed on'. Of these there were the boys who had to get qualifications which would lead to a job such as teaching. Then there were the academics. I just wanted to get to university. Inspired by Bob Williams, I wanted the flat, the parties, the lifestyle and the kudos that came with being a student. I didn't care if it never got me anywhere near a job. I fancied myself as Kirkby's answer to Jack Kerouac and nothing was getting in my way.

Although violence between the boys of St Kevins and those of Roughwood had been rumoured before we arrived at the school, there was nothing more than minor skirmishes in the time that I was there. I think that both schools had made arrangements to stagger starting and closing times to reduce the likelihood of any shenanigans. However there were repeated 'rumours of war'. These usually involved the notion that some gang or other were 'coming down' to cause mayhem. The kids most often thought to be coming down were kids from the neighbouring township of Croxteth (known as Crocky). How the marauding hordes were supposed to get from Crocky to Kirkby was never explained. Just the transport logistics of bringing marauding hordes up the East Lancs road would have been formidable. Their motivation for coming to inflict ultra violence on us was never clarified either. They were on their way and that was enough for mass hysteria. The effects of these events on the school should not be minimised. Teachers would have to take measures to make sure that boys were not grouping outside the school to fight off the invading multitudes. Rumours and fake news would accompany these mass panics. 'Can your mum sew?' one boy was rumoured to have been asked 'Yes' replied the poor sap. 'Well get her to stitch that' the Crockyite was supposed to have said, slashing his poor, innocent victim with a blade.

I later discovered that many parts of Liverpool had their own versions of this story and these events. But in these other versions it would be Kirkby kids who were coming down, frequently naming Saint Kevins boys as the source of the mayhem. They had nothing to fear from me. I had to get home for my tea.

Sex and the single school boy

"Masturbatio est abusus cupiditatum naturalium. Sexus fit ad matrimonium et solum matrimonium". Translated from 'My Catholic Life, a story of personal conversion'.

On the way to school me and my friends used to play marbles, or 'ollies'. This was a game played in the gutters of the roads. We had no fear of being hit by a vehicle; there were so few on the road. This was not the game as played on TV or in films, with a circle and a hole in the middle. No, ours was a horizontal game. We rolled the olly along the gutter and the next player would try to hit it by rolling along another. Low currency ollies were made of glass and you could buy them by the packet in the newsagents. The more unusual the look of the olly, the higher its trade value. Highest value ollies were called 'steelies' and were just round ball bearings, probably obtained from somewhere on the industrial estate. The greater the size, the bigger the value. There were also bearings in a cylindrical shape called for some reason 'German steelies'. These were great as trading items but they were rubbish as ollies. They would not roll, so you couldn't use them in battle to any effect.

But I digress. One day on the way to school I noticed a group of girls who had been in my class in junior school. They were off to the girls RC school twinned with us, Saint Gregorys. Something had changed, something big. While we looked like characters from some 'Just William' spin off, they looked like they were on their way to a nightclub. We looked like kids. They looked like women. Things were underway.

Looking back, you would have to say that sex was not handled well in our single sex Roman Catholic school, surprisingly enough. Or rather, it was barely handled at all. This is surprising too, because the anti sex objections of the Catholic church to the direction of travel in society was well known. Given the papal hostility to contraception and the in principle objection to the 1967 abortion act, one might have expected the school to attempt to drill us in Catholic orthodoxy. But by the time our voices began to drop it was rather the other way around. We used Catholic teaching in these matters as another front on which we could challenge the staff.

Nobody liked dealing with these matters in response. The secular teachers, very few of whom had the ten children families, didn't like to talk about it. Their parents and grandparents had huge families but science had given them the opportunity to limit the size of theirs, and they took it. But the religious teachers likewise had moderately sized families. If they only had three kids there was only two explanations: they were defying the Pope or marital relations had ceased to be. There was no middle way that did not involve some sort of pathology. The celibate priests didnt find the subject any easier to talk about either. What could they have to contribute to the discussion? Some of the lads had more carnal knowledge than they did, in theory at least.

As for the actual facts of life, this was not a subject which was visited with any regularity and from a pedagogical point of view, was always handled badly. I recall one occasion when we were all (I seem to remember it was scores of us) gathered in the main school hall where a health visitor (I think!) had to tell us what was going on in our gonads from the lectern that Mr Moorhead usually delivered his announcements from. It was a disaster from every point of view. The one good thing about this event was that her talk was listened to in absolute, deathly silence. A teacher could always get this sort of quiet if they ever visited the subject of sex in class. I never actually saw this myself, but I am certain that even a student teacher could have quelled the noise in class by this ruse. So, although the poor lady was listened to in silence, under the surface things did not go well. In my group the embarrassment was running so intensely that everyone was giggling like idiots. I myself had a school bag that ever after bore the teeth marks I bit into its strap during this session to try to stop myself laughing. Anything that helped me control the embarrassed laughter that my mates' heaving shoulders had set off, I would try: biting my lip, pinching my leg, you name it.

In any case, the amateur sexologists of the school yard had pretty much kept us up to speed with the grim but strangely compelling facts of life. We had a rough and ready grasp of the main points even by the end of the second year. If any visual aids were required we could always consult those encyclopaedias of female anatomy, the underwear sections of mail order catalogues. Here stout ladies of a certain age, bearing some resemblance to the lady health visitor as I recall, would demonstrate the latest in foundation garments. This was not the skimpy lingerie of later years, to be sure, but they did give us food for thought. The Littlewoods catalogue was not the exclusive source of this source of information. One lad in our class claimed that he knew the days on which the mannequins in the shop windows of Oakes and Hulme in the townie had their outfits changed. He said that he would wait outside to see the lady models stripped of their clothes, layer by layer. It was not me. I did not go there. There are limits.

Among the boys there was a lively currency in whatever erotic materials that were available. I don't recall any erotic novels doing the rounds. That would take too much concentration and application. But there was widespread circulation of pictures. Early on this would be restricted to the 'girly' magazines of the period. A magazine called Parade was the top seller in this market. Compared with what came later, Parade was innocence itself, although it did feature limited female nudity. The magazines which made it to school were often found on the way to school in bushes. There was an enormous amount of this type of material thrown away, presumably in fear of wives or mothers catching it on the person of the purchaser. So, the patchy theoretical aspects of human reproduction were supplemented by the images and stories obtained from the hedgerows of the town. The internet has caused the mass extinction of this sort of material. One day, someone turned up with a crumpled sheet that had been found in one of these hedges. It indicated that there was a possibility, no more than that, that ladies had hair 'down there'. This was headline news for a week.

Occasionally one would hear of boys and girls trapped by their own reproductive organs into unwanted marriages. On this the rules were clear. If you got a girl pregnant you were not to leave her 'in the lurch'. The decent thing was to 'stand by' her. I can't imagine how much marital misery these assumptions must have caused, or how many of my school chums had entered the world via one of these dismal arrangements.

If sexual development was rough and ready for straight kids in Saint Kevins I cant imagine what life was like for gay kids. I did not know of any kids, not even one, that I knew or suspected of being gay. Not a single one. I am guessing that there was at least one gay kid in my class, there must have been. But neither then or subsequently has anyone come out of the closet. Life must have been terrifying for them and the fear of exposure a feature of their daily lives. In 1966 when we arrived in Saint Kevins, homosexuality had only been decriminalised for three years. And the attitude of the church to gay lifestyle was (and is) well known, although as I recall, they didn't go on about it much in school. They were probably too embarrassed to talk about that too. Whatever the attitude of the Church, if I had been gay at that time, among those boys, I would have kept my trap shut too. Inclusive, it wasn't.

Any of the activities that teenage boys get up to under the bed clothes were banned by the church but in subtle, understated ways. There were not many mentions of how bad 'acts of self pollution' were from the school and religious hierarchy, but we all knew the score. They didn't press the point but we all knew that the quickest way to make baby Jesus cry was to 'relax in a gentleman's way'.

When we were sixteen or so there was an interesting development. I am not alone in recalling this episode. If I was, it might be dismissed as a flight of schoolboy fantasy, but this recollection has been confirmed by everyone in my class who I am still in contact with. Waiting to go into the school blocks for lessons (staying inside school blocks during breaks was strictly forbidden, unless there was torrential rain) the boys would be required to stand in straight, quiet lines. We would face a staircase running up the three floors of the school. One side of the staircase was glass fronted, the side we queued on. Every time we queued up outside that block a teacher, a young woman teacher, an attractive young woman teacher in one of those very mini skirts that were all young women wore then, would walk up the staircase and look down on the love lorne masses. The queues would go quiet as the boys stared back at her in quiet adoration. Thank you Miss, wherever you are now.

In terms of mixing with the opposite sex, well, before sixth form there wasn't much to be honest. There were discos in the Labour club which were interesting enough. But serious parties had to wait until we were old enough to make out we were entitled to buy alcohol. The first house party I went to was opposite the school. I don't recall whose house it was in. It was a strange affair, and many of the people I didn't know. In fact I dont know how I came to be there. But when the lights were turned off, there was a sort of scrum in the room with strangers locking gobs with each other. Strangest parties I ever went to.

By the time we got to the sixth form, matters had relaxed to a considerable degree, sexwise (take that, Charlie). By now there were semi timetabled mixing sessions between the sixth forms of St Kevins and our twin, female school St Gregorys. After six years of gender segregation we now swam in very different waters. We used to organise dances in our sixth form base. I recall a hugely successful one where we booked a band called 'Glass Dream'. I wonder what happened to them? Hardest game in the world, show business.

As sixth form wore on our extracurricular activities consisted to a great extent in doing voluntary work in a charming Kirkby institution known as the Falcon. Barely legal, we would help the staff shift prodigious volumes of booze from behind the bar to the gents toilets, laying our wallets and our kidneys at the disposal of the staff. This caused me some problems. My dad was a teetotaller. Not your average teetotaller either. It wasn't that he didn't like drink (which he didn't). Rather, he saw drink as a conspiracy organised by the Conservative Party to keep workers skint so they'd work for nothing. He couldn't get his head around why working men would rather sit in the boozer than be at home with their families. Or, better, going to union meetings. I asked him once what he would do if he ever got booze banned. Joking, he said 'I'm going to start on telly'

He couldn't have been best pleased when I started coming home from the Falcon smelling of booze. But youth must have its day, Da! And besides, the Falcon was opposite Saint Gregory's girl's school, so it was handy for our new chums in their sixth form.

The girls we met in Saint Gregorys and the impressions that they made on us were very profound. When us old lags get together, we still talk in sentimental terms about the girls who were our favourites and who shaped our thinking. Many of my class (at least four) met and married girls from this group and all of them are married still.

I have no idea what became of the gay lads.

This sporting life

'I can't feel my hands or feet or flesh at all, like I'm a ghost who wouldn't know the earth was under him if he didn't see it now and again through the mist.' Alan Sillitoe, The Loneliness of the Long Distance Runner

I hated sport in school and I still do in life. Watching it is bad enough but doing sport is purgatory to me. This was not a popular stance in a boys school of the size of Saint Kevins. There was no anti sport faction you could join. The closest you came to an anti sport body of opinion was the asthmatics and neurotics, and they resented their exclusion from all the grunting and sweating that was going on fieldwise (your move, Charlie!). I hated everything about it: the changing rooms with their bouquet of rubber and boy sweat. I hated being out in the cold with only the mud for comfort. Out chasing a ball in the bleak midwinter, possibly in the rain, was about as far from my vision of contentment as it was possible to get. The other lads loved it, that's what I could never understand. Lining up to get into the changing rooms the teachers could say 'You're only losing time on the pitch lads!' and there would be instant order. Only talking about sex had a faster response. Their enthusiasm was boundless. But not me. I hated it.

It might have been because I don't think I have ever been a team player. And sharing showers with a gang of adolescent lads was way too teamy for me. There were lads in class who were, shall we say, further along in their pubertal journey than me and boy, did they let you know. 'Yes George, very impressive, now dry it off and put it away'. Even now, Eeeeuuw.

If you want a picture of me on the 1970s field of sport, think of the scenes in Kes where Billy Caspar, the sport-hostile underachiever, is climbing up the goalposts as the balls are going into the goal he is supposed to be defending. That was me, only without the urge to climb the posts.

When we first went up to St Kevs we were expected to bring our own kits and naturally the kids bought the colours of the teams they supported; mostly Liverpool kits with a smattering of Everton. As a comment on this nonsense I picked the team that was lowest in the league and picked their kit. It was Wolves. I wore that kit, not the teams kit, the actual kit until the fifth year when I retired from the world of sport entirely.

No, how I saw myself was entirely different from my hard tackling contemporaries. I saw myself as an aesthete, a budding Wilde. A sensitive type 'who cries, he knows not why'. This was a million miles from my mudstained mates. A gentle soul, I would not be trampled under the studs of these sportniks. My mind would be on higher things: the poems of Catullus, the prospects for Socialist transformation of society and the lingerie section of the Freemans catalogue. I was a poet and all this sport was prose. Mud spattered, freezing cold prose oh, and by the way lads, the hot water's off so you'll have to get a cold shower.

And don't run away with the idea that this disinterest was a passive reluctance to participate. This was an active, in your face refusal to have-a-go. Firstly it spread from footy to all other sports, in the case of St Kevins, running (what on earth is the point?) to cricket and rugby. St Kevins had a healthy sub culture of rugby football which was overshadowed by regular footy. One of the lads in our sixth form went on to play for St Helen's, or something, I'm sketchy on the details. For myself I only ever played one game of rugby, and I spent the entire game running away from the ball. Bad things happened to boys who went near the ball. They got trampled by stampedes of other boys. As a minimum I feared getting wet. On a freezing November morning this was a fate worse than death to me.

Myself and my mate would compete to be picked last in the gruesome beauty contests that was the picking. Who could resist me, I would wonder, standing shivering and resentful in my shrunken Wolves kit? We would wait as our fellows would be chosen, past the diabetics, past the asthmatics, past the nail biters until there was only us two left. My partner in crime would later go over to the other side and become a sport enthusiast, but I have long forgiven him this act of desertion. On the field of play itself we would play a parallel game to the rest of the lads. Tom had a nice line in sarcastic commentary on the quality of the play whenever the teachers got hold of the ball: 'Good pass, sir', 'Well thought through sir', 'Excellent decision, sir'. I mean, the teacher could hardly complain about being praised, could he? For myself I would stand around refusing to run, in striking distance of the goal. When the ball came anywhere near me I would use my legs, fresh from not running, to toe end the ball in for an entirely undeserved goal. The rest of the workhorses who wore themselves out running could not have taken kindly to this unmerited glory. But what could they say? It was a win win situation if ever there was one. If ever I got bored with this I would pop one into my own net just to spice things up. This did nothing for team spirit and only had the effect of making me even less popular next time it came to team picking time.

In the fifth year I became what was known technically to the gym fraternity as a non kitter. 'Could all the non kitters come out to the front please' and we would be segregated from the rest of the lads who by now would be chomping at the bit to get muddy. In one period of liberalisation we were allowed to take ourselves off to any empty room we could find and get on with things. This used to mean listening to the radio, talking about music or reading the texts set for our up and coming O levels. One of these was 'Sons and Lovers' by DH Lawrence. Frankly, I would rather have been playing footy than reading that miserable get, but beggars can't be choosers.

Eventually a new regime came in which was not satisfied with this arrangement. Even they recognised that they could not force the non kitters to come in equipped for the track and field. But neither was the new authoritarianism prepared to tolerate wholesale desertion from the pitches. We were forced to stand by the side of the pitches and watch the 'Man on!', 'Square ball!' antics of our fellows, even in the rain. It left me longing to score a blinder one more time, right in the back of my own net. Not that we had nets.

Academic Affairs

"Candidates do well in examinations from various reasons, some from genuine ability, obviously, but others because doing well in examinations is what they do well; they can put on a show" Alan Bennett, 'The History Boys'

As soon as I laid off fancying myself as a train driver or a superhero, I wanted to be a student. Student life had everything I wanted. Away from Kirkby, in my own flat with people from different parts of the country and paid to read. A new academic career in a new town and a big fat qualification at the end. Not only that, there was rebellion. Militant students were on the march. Student sit-ins in the nation's art colleges were still a thing and the whole scene had the glamour of sticking it to the Man.

This was a period where only 5% of the population as a whole went into higher education and that is a measure across the country as a whole. In Kirkby I am guessing that this figure was considerably lower. Nobody in my family had ever been to university, although I cannot say that I didn't know anybody from Kirkby who had gone down that route. Our next door neighbour's son, some years older than me, had gone to the London School of Economics and I recall him talking to my dad over the fence about the turmoil in his department. He went on to become a university professor in his own right, Professor Tom Cannon. Listening to him chatting strengthened my resolve to go. When it came time for applying to university, he came into our house and chatted me through the interview process and gave me some tips about how I might approach my own; what names to drop and so on.

I had all this figured out well before we set about our studies for 'O' level GCEs. I chose my subjects with the goal of a university application in mind. They were to neatly dovetail with my A level GCEs in two year's time and would constitute the poker hand of qualifications I would require for my application form. So imagine my surprise when the careers master sat me down, with my mum and dad in attendance behind me and said words to the effect of 'Well yes. O levels certainly. We'll see about A levels later'. I was outraged. Not in front of him, obviously. But, the way I saw it, he was pouring cold water on my only ambition in life. Outraged, I tell you.

But looking back my view has softened. At first I took this as being evidence of a culture of low expectation. I saw it as saying that lads from our school should limit their ambitions and be prepared to narrow their horizons. But with the maturity of years I have come to a different view.

Somebody from a Facebook group about Kirkby history posted a list of the teachers from the Saint Kevins of my generation. This was interesting enough. But it also listed the educational backgrounds of the teachers named. Many of the teachers had pretty underwhelming educational backgrounds of their own and many looked as though they had gone into teaching after leaving the army with little more than lived experience to guide them. Teaching was desperately short of recruits at the time as I recall. Also, even within my mates, some very capable kids who could easily have gone down the university route did not make it through to A levels. In many cases the temptation of high wages, secure jobs and romance outweighed the attractions of varsity life. The things that attracted me would be poison to them. Whatever else it had to say for itself, a student's life was a one way ticket to poverty, scruffdom and not getting your round in. It wasnt for everyone. In fact I had to have a lot of conversations with lads who thought I was nuts for even thinking about it. And when I told them what I was going to study, that clinched it: philosophy. 'What are you going to do with that then?' expressed in a mocking voice was a question I heard so often that I developed a stock answer: 'Think clearly'.

Many years later and after training to be a nurse (where my degree, any degree, would guarantee success for your application) and then training to be a nurse teacher, this philosophy degree turned out to be an actual career move. In the mid 1980s there was an explosion of interest across all of the healthcare professions in the subject of ethics in health care: who should get the last kidney machine, was it ever justifiable to end someone's life who is in pain and wishes to die, you get the sort of thing. This put me in an enviable position to pursue fascinating subjects and get paid for it. But I digress.

I don't know what the kids in the other streams used to make of us in the 'academic' streams. After all, we were from the same roads as them, we ate with them at dinner times and we shared the same house groups as them. I do not recall any systematic hostility from the rest of the school except for one occasion. We were leaving the arts block and going to our next lessons. There were other kids waiting to go in, lined up in queues. They started to chant 'Fruits, Fruits, Fruits' at us. We ignored it and passed by, end of anecdote. The word 'Fruit' when applied to you in the St Kevins of the 1960s did not have any of the overtones of homosexuality that the word came to carry later. It meant rather a teacher's pet, a goody two shoes geek, a pal of Lord Snooty. So it was still fighting talk, not in my case obviously, but certainly in the case of one of our mates who knew his way around a fracas. To this day I wonder if those kids know how thin the ice was they were stomping on.

At some point in our middle school period, about 1968-69, the school obtained a computer. It would be hard to exaggerate the reverence which this piece of kit commanded. We were invited to come to admire it in the main hall, and we were drilled in how to input stuff into its mighty brain before we were introduced to it. And indeed, it was impressive and could do calculations. It was blue as I recall. It didn't have the luxury of a screen or anything fancy like that. In fact it jotted its conclusions on the sort of paper roll that came out of tills, or bus tickets. Come to think of it, it worked like an atom age adding machine. I think that today it would probably be one of those programmable calculators, only without the display function. I never got the hang of them either. It was said to have cost the school a mint of money. I bet that, after a few years of obsolescence, it was put into a skip. I equally suspect that now it would be an object of historical interest and would be, once again, worth a mint.

Early doors computer studies wasn't the only field in which our school enthusiastically adopted the modern. It was an early adopter of Nuffield approaches to education. This required us to learn by doing. Gone were the boring old requirements to learn stuff by rote. No, with Nuffield physics you could arse around with kit making patterns and creating waves in water and the learning would just slide in unnoticed. We had two subjects where these educational experiments were inflicted on us: physics and, of all things, Latin. In physics, all I can recall were these machines that made waves in water and allowed us to create interference patterns. And that's all I can remember of O level physics, apart from some other stuff I shouldn't raise in polite company. But in Latin I have more of a recollection. Up to Nuffield Latin we were drilled in Latin verbs and declensions. I can still recite them: amo, amas, amat and mensa, mensa, mensam etc respectively. They were solidly learned, by whatever definition of learning you wish to choose. Then came Nuffield Latin. Put away those text books kids! We have got Latin comics! So out came these orange booklets with pictures of waving characters: 'Hic est pater!'. They went on to little storylines about life on a Roman farm. My learning came to a halt right there, even though I got low grade passes at O level in both physics and Latin. I cant imagine how I managed this, and I wonder about the quality of the exam to be honest

As well as showing us around quadratic equations and Latin declensions, St Kevins was also keen to show us the skills we might need in life, at least in the years before O level. The skills we were shown in these years were all aimed at man type activities. These were the years before second wave feminism, so they were unembarrassed by gender stereotyping. We were shown woodwork and metalwork for the budding carpenters and engineers among us. I was hopeless at both. We were supposed to be making little objects in class and I always fell very far behind. I might have been an embarrassment to my dad, a joiner, if it wasn't for the fact that he hated being a manual worker and wanted me to stay far away from that type of work. There was a kid in my class who was off for ages and ages with TB or something. But when he came back he was still further along with his 'condiment holder' or whatever we were supposed to be making. This disinclination to manual labour has stood me in good stead all my life and the letters DIY stand for Don't Involve Yourself in my head.

The one skill I would have appreciated learning at this time was firmly sectioned off by the stereotyping of the day. I would have found an ability to type to be a tremendous value in my life. At university, and subsequently in my job an ability to touch type would have been a key skill for me. I still can't type properly, even after years of typing with two fingers. But in those days typing = secretarial = women. No ifs or buts.

Learning to type would have been like cross dressing to school.

As for where we studied after school, most of the mates I kept in touch with went into teacher training. Another lad went on to become a prominent Merseyside architect. I don't know what happened to the rest. For the final year of school I stayed in my bedroom and worked like I have never worked before or since. When the A level results came out I was tense as hell. Going up to school to get the results, Elmer Fudd approached me and said 'Don't worry, you've done well' and indeed I had obtained the grades I needed to reach escape velocity from Kirkby. A couple of my mates went back to college and got their grades a couple of years later. In fact they studied under my future father in law in Liverpool Central College, the wonderful Jimmy Rand. He was himself a late convert to higher education, having traded in his brickie's trowel for an academic gown when he was in his forties.

Epilogue: the escape

"No lad who has liberty for the first time, and twenty pounds in his pocket, is very sad, and Chris rode towards Bangor thinking not so much of the kind mother left alone, and of the home behind him, but of tomorrow, and all the wonders it would bring." Paraphrased from William Makepeace Thackeray's 'Barry Lyndon'

In 1973 with four A levels in my possession I left Saint Kevins and by October of that year I was settling into life in Bangor. Driving away in the taxi I looked back on the only home I had ever known where my mother was gently weeping on the step and I was overjoyed, as harsh as that might sound. And, thanks to Tom Moynihan's advice and Bob Williams' inspiration I was about to spend three of the best years I ever lived in Gogledd Cymru. I spent my final year in a cottage at the mouth of the Llanberis valley, with a view of Snowdon. Freezing, yes, but blissful. My mates from school all stayed in touch and came to visit me with some regularity. Here they are abusing the hospitality of the area on Bangor Mountain

But as the years went by we all lost touch, what with the demands of work and family. It's a common enough story I suppose. But by the miracle of modern social media we have all got together again and regularly squander what is left of our cognitive ability by consuming, frankly, foolish amounts of alcohol (see illustration below). But as I tell myself the morning after our get togethers, at least it's not crack cocaine.

The year is 2022. Older, yes but possibly not wiser. Wish you were still here Phil Donnelly.

Printed in Great Britain
by Amazon